A Season Wild

Selected Poems

Lana Wolkonsky

For My Husband and Children

Contents

He who binds to himself a joy
does the winged life destroy;
but he who kisses the joy as it flies
lives in eternity's sun rise.

Eternity
William Blake

I went to the woods because I wished to live
deliberately, to front only the essential facts of life,
and see if I could not learn what it had to teach,
and not, when I came to die, discover that I had
not lived.

Walden
Henry David
Thoreau

Of Goodness Known

A table set by Christ's own honor;
Sat the lone, few brothers—hearts
Of solid intellect and worldly wit;
Their pride be known, their
Reverence aside: to medley
Dreams on southern end and
'Round the gilt remembrance
Sipped from chalice pure.

Our language spoke a verbal pride,
Did soft redeem our facile host and
His adoring insight into all so tangible,
So real—his manner just; his quiet,
Piercing way, his eloquent appeal
Does surface as it does surpass
These boundaries once
Styled in varied way.

In modest realm, in regal soul, in
Sacred touch we wished no more
That night for so entrusted we
Became at these immeasurable
Truths that (sung before us)
Carved a means to justice won,
To all-embracing unity of force
Endeared by gentle voice, by
Power's thrust, of goodness known.

Sweet friend this evening shared and
So became a witness to the solid, most
Unending faith your life's own calling
Matches—none can be this individual,
Most poignant grace which yours alone
No rivals has. Your Eminence, in goodness
Do you shine and that immovable belief
That is the very core of virtue's realm.

On Freedom's
Way

There, outside—where colors fade
As tears roll soiled to bring each
Sharpened edge, each hollow wound
To sound recall, to blinded trust; the
Side once known in constant presence,
Steel and burn a passed glance—
On freedom's way, on savior's will.

Now realized laughter gone, a wish,
A turn, a living gesture such did
Bring again this bitter taste:
This long-unheard, stern voice.
How think it void—when once a part,
It reigns for all days here as unifying nerve.

Did blinded walk in pure, green, floral fields
On amber afternoons of beauty lights to think
Alone, this gone might be—in lost belief a
Cinder perished stands a fortress in one heart.

The mind that chose togetherness unite;
Is on its way, on freedom's way—
So uncontrolled all else should
Stand akin to these uncharted,
Unrehearsed displeasures.

Drive the win when lost will be
The soul's unbidding keys: to lie
In resource pure, an innocence
Can stand or be so tolerated thus;
In eagles' eye a harnessed fill of
Last time felt—when in this belly
Life did churn, then also rivaled
Flesh did punctuate through a shadowed,
Pained emotion and turn its back so true.

Such passages may not yet be in
Civil understandings but hidden
In a better hand. That hand which
Not upon the counter slammed,
That hand which did not soft
Embrace in human deed, that hand—
That hidden hand which only raises
Light onto a faceless treasure.

And forgives those not endowed
By glory on a day forsaken, on a night
Worth less than all that stood before;
And death—in most alluring affirmation
Passes-by again, as some (in hope) do perish.

Desired Fate

Bleak this day that wakes me
In a swollen pride—the faded
Dunes and desolate grey outside
Are null compared to my heart's
Walk along the beaches of desired
Fate; such trivial times, when
Of the splendid past we sing:
The only praises gone (to fetch a
Scoundrel new) do separate us
As they do unite our will.

O up-coming folly—
Upon the branches limp
A rotted relic hangs and
Digs us deep into the watery
Confusion life can bring.

Up, on tops of mountains bold,
A new endeavour as the
Challenged peak—bare and
Monstrous, stares us down into
Our soggy earth—drenched with
All we are, with all we know.
Then stand, a tribute lone to
Harboured outcome—now
In this culmination rise
To face another day.

In still-untangled justice steer
The way to sobered truth, to
Turn of such events most
Unpredictable to some—
Yearn through these such
Seeded, vying visions to
Renew a close perfection.

One we read and one
Believed, one encountered
On the road now closed; so
Take an alternate construction
Route to pass the day, to quiet
Pull into the drives of man.

Eternal Sky

Such perfect lights, that
Cast out on a shadowy sea,
Do beam across this slate—
Eternal sky. Eternal dream,
Eternal resurrection only
Of a likeness found.

Now cast forgiveness on
This world, now paint a
Second vision to my name
And leave this dying earth
To sleep a season wild, to
Wake in earnest pleasure—
Then to fall again
In prize of man.

Such thoughts today will
Pass: when cold stillness
Sets into the hardened soil
And reaps a loss; a sleeping,
Tender loss unknown—we
Meet on future transits to
The favored life beyond.

*Does
Forgiveness
Lie*

To look—out into the soft, abundant
Pleasures and watch the merry streak
Of life just pass me by; it wishes as the
Loneful dreamer, of a promised kingdom found.

I sleep the gentle, moving whispers—
Gone into the tepid night; as on the
Edge of mindful reason saddened
Sits the fruit of man. Alone, we
All must face our fading, fleshy luck;
In streams across the sky, a colored wave—
Resembling likenesses of images once
Seen in long-imagined, now-forgotten
Patches been. When even to the ends of
Every knowledge, every breath—in
True unification do we pass, still there:
Along the blue uncharted, does forgiveness lie.

Now worried, never late we wished
These promises—now spill our earthly
Goodness fair to last until that breath,
That final respiration past.

Once Known

Whose heart you beat—
The range you feel, the
Strength you keep;
Endeavours bare once
Known to steal in
Earthly nights, in
Quiet feel so fond.

I rage to know our bets,
Placed so to weave the
Night with me most fair,
In trial still I stand and
Watch your iron will with
Pride; to know such beast,
To kindly, soft embrace a
Warmth but given to that
Seed before, that fleshful
Love without the hard
Today I savour so.

Of Opposing Cause

Clear it folds to see,
That door which closes
Now on liberty—same
As once it opened all
A private field and
Passport mine it was.

Love then flourished on
Sweet harmony; shut now
But in annoyance on my being.
These fragrant moments
Noise on me exude and
Cost again in doubled verse
What left to feel in bare
Arrest is mine.

O troubled soul—fear not
A conquest or a judgment:
These invisible transparencies
Are close to touch and in
Their smoothness buried do
They my weakness keep.

Smile to me, you burnished charmer;
With steely eye in fervent rest, you
Delve not on this sphere I listen and
In our differences we weep together
Of opposing cause.

*A Coveted
Adorn*

For all your love,
For all your grace
There is no jewel
That can embrace
Beyond a coveted adorn,
Inside the tremors
Of this heart.

Still stern and sure,
Your quiet way is
Mine for time ahead—
When in each gesture,
Each reply; the humble
Truth does ring.

When some your
Rules cannot comply
With reason firm, no
Judgment made, no
Saddened state can
Re-attest a passing whim.

Smile free, O savior
Mine and in such warm,
Enamoured faith do shine.

Confirmed

Lying in a golden, shiny
Yellow broth—a bath
So subtle-warm that it
Did conjure-up the senses
Once, when laden with a
Second child in earnest
Flesh did sing. A perfumed,
Soft refrain still lingers to the
Touch of distant song and
Hidden verse in all this
Trembling rush of worldly things.

How strange the day
When noticeable change
Does overtake the youthly glow,
As in a solemn night all same in
Blinded vision calls; the touch
Remains a sense's limb, that
Strong repeals our virtue's skin.
Stray cold into uncharted thought—
The craving lessened, sorrow keeps;
A faltered try out-shines this grief
And each beginning tales does bury
Deeper to an ending boundary
Of steepened justice.

The Wish

To shut these smaller
Eyes and sleep—a
Distant promise did it
Keep when said a lost
Emotion perished in an
Unknown, weeping rest.

No trust today in falling
Spirit, no soft repute;
Still feathered whispers
'Cross the angered
Sky do streak.

No wish is made, no
Promise broken—none this
Fascinating rhyme can wipe
The words already spoken.

So silence keep and dreams
Within revert, to saddened
Wishes life converts—breathe
The winter's dark, sweet
Air and bid farewell
To summer's fare.

Nature's Sleep

The muted silence of this
Long, enduring realm of
Cold; when fields lie still,
Blanketed in constant snows
And on this soul a frozen hatred
Knocks—breaking the intoxicated
Freedom of a fanciful, a dancing spring.

Ahead, the mountains in
Mysterious allure do reach
To touch the still, grey skies
And taught alone within a nature's
Thrust, a managed will; craved to find
Our solace in deep, bundled peace—
Some sleeping stranger passed in vision nights.

Arose in mornings thunder,
As the quiet rains did fall;
Awake did stretched recline
To listen and to feel those winds
Pass through the very thin of life.

When Winter Comes

Outside the frost will blow—
And blow my heart's sweet
Will away; on angry days, in
Chance so unfulfilled yet free:
The land may shadow on these
Most material concessions to
Reveal the soul of justice true.

To hide the crinkled, written
Face that time won't hide, that
Restoration even cannot change—
The few, tame tries an open heart
May sing; this reigning wisdom
Drew another image, bannered
Now along the once-eternal shore
Of hungry truth, of yearning
Knowledge, of acquired
Information lost in clamour
This world knows too well.

When winter comes these
Dreams may change—to
Leave the vacant spirit wild
On dessert plains, on soft
Reflection's edge; some timid
Tries at consolation might
True encourage honorable fate
And cheer forgiveness on.

In frozen passion mingled
With a slaty steel, there found
Will be in downtown dirt a lost,
Artistic seed. From it our coldnesses
Will chide and in the quiet deaths
Our degradation's search will end
In secret passage to a foolish spring.

In thought, in dreams—still buried by
A snow-layed edge; as reason calls,
As trembling life hangs on to every
Breath, these seasonal rebutes arrive
In tow and we a shovel then in hand
Shall take to listen while the dawn's
Crisp rattling wakes our senses.

On Passing
Moons

How could one miss be called
This hour, when tranquil in
An amber gaze, the sun casts
Lonely passion on the earth
And beauty, dream-like falls
Into a shadowy display.

Our years leave faded joy
Across the faces—where
Angered bliss and we, like
Harmony forgotten; ride
On passing moons away;
Leaving love to once-known
Strangers now. Such confidences
Broken, stand in frozen try, in
Dreamy death to smooth away
The years and call it done.

Imagination's Course

In warm, sweet sleep I go
Through colonnades of whispers
To a tropical enchantment
On some placid shore,
Where angels sweep
The sapphire skies and
Liquid onyx waters bathe.

Where perfect moons
Each night appear
To light the even
Bronze of day aglow—
Across O beauty's fleshy palette.
Breezes pure and soft as life's
Most delicate elixir flow—
They pass above a naked skin
To leave imagination's course
In tranquil dream.

I wake to frozen rains,
To late the sun does rise,
To early darkness: to winter's flame;
In rising I again do find
The summer rose (still live)
In fragrant stillness there—
Standing near the broken glass,
The first of snows that fall this day.

He gathers at his table round,
A flavourful, a varied set;
His presence made—a
Knowledge vast, an
Intellect profound
Out-lasts us all and
Days like these we
Cherish wildly in
His company to
Shine, to keep.

Solemn pasts, as tributes strong
Can ours be for days to come—
On early rise in morning's sight,
On eerie nights in dismal
Light of grey we praise his way,
His soft, uncompromising will
And steely trust, O friend of mine!

*Tomorrow's
Shoot*

The arch and bow have given way—
The hare, the buck, the sweet
Stench of fowl that falls
In showers from the sky,
Then lands in padded thumps
Around a sagey brush with
Hounds-a-howling brisk in tow;
To raise a brow with feathers
Low and tangle in a new found
Skin on chilling stages, twisted vine.
We grapes of promises do keep—
Outside these drives and virtues reap.

Final Sun

Bloodied feathers fall to
Grace our land already coloured
With the holly and a cherry red of
Cartridges once full.

The fetch is made—
Still warm a pheasant's heart
Does beat and beaters 'round
With yells collect (to gather-up)
This glory turn, this final sun.

Passed Free

Another moon, another life
That passes for our eye to see—
Replenished in a careful
Harmony of time, of light, of
Grateful satisfaction; you, our
Host, so regal prize has made
Each breath a lasting thought,
Each sigh—relief, each wish
Yet more-encompassing reality
Of this, a most exquisite day:
Passed free in gentle heart,
In rare precision, in an act
Of careful undertakings and a
Good night sleep shall rest
Replenish every sense to make
Us willing for another day.

*Brown-Eyed
Lab*

The smell of sweetness quartered
By a spike of gin and tremble not,
My fairness treat—a level love
Of air when leashed reply in
Muscled form repeats a steady
Hand with berried shrub surround.

The icy creek in fairness clear
Sounds shimmer by direction's
Antiquated stare; she wiggles to
A climb and raises furred,
Those perfect brows.

My stranger's pet, my lone
Contender grace does bear
It well through years' outlined,
Rehearsed, fine-worked: in
Luxury of peace then layed
to rest—to followed be by
Breeder's dream and
Trainer's trust, stern hand.

Hit

Struggling in the boggy
Brush, my fine, enchanted
Feathered fowl—this foul
Amusement none; of man's
One heartless game: the
Gain is rung in silvered horn
And such this day begun.

*Beyond Us
Willed*

May in the innocence of love
This heart received be, as
It upon you had been set;
Unknown to me, beyond my
Fleshy will: for long, for
All eternity perhaps—then
To its blessing we succumb,
To live now with a full emotion.

Fill this house with laughter;
Tears and joy will ours be for
All these days ahead: when
We together sit and pray
Thanksgiving for these deeds
That so beyond us willed.

Together now—remember love
Which started in the heart and
So for life shall guide our
Senses, as the mind does
Follow its own way.

The End

Phone receiver down:
A click was heard;
This conversation ended
Un-resolved (as many have).

None will follow, yet
The solemn drama lives
And winds these times
Into a soft aggression.

Strong the language thus
And so infallible it goes,
Our sweetened destinies—
The bitter pill now
Passed and over with.

A Leave

Into a winter darkness bare
You go, ride-off into a
Setting light to leave me
Broken with a tear, a
Heart in saddened
State suppressed
And life so quartered,
Nothing moves to
Limit this reply.

You go—a leave with
Which a piece of
Happiness does
Leave as well; a
Chilling dream, a
Real forgiveness felt.

What seen remains is
But a distant diesel gone
Along a shadowed highway
And the city waits for you,
My two alone; a part of me—
My two, so gone you go
Into the night without a tow
This time—leaving trust
And memory behind
With us to writhe, to hurt,
To tremble lonely in our
Own unknown, in our
Darknesses, in our light.

Because tomorrow brings such
Challenges, still you dare to
Make your lasting imprint ours
And we figure and we think.

Tonight the night is ours
As we hurt by you this
Time; we so surrender
Peace, we pain, we shine.

Earnest Day

When all the world does stop
To so endear this gracious
Season's bliss, the trembling
Heart pronounces love in
Varied senses—as an
Outward kiss may often
Seem loud, sweet folly;
So my Lord does reign
In milder vision on
This, most gloried day.

To you these praises go
And raise a goblet pure,
While frozen rains may
Fall and wash away
A myriad of keen
Remembrance.

Earnest day it is, O singled,
Saintly wisdom such; as only
You, most treasured friend
Might have. Bless now your
Fruit and wish upon the only
Wishes you (surrounded by an
Army of devoted hearts) may
Want; our time together rich
And few, a petty world cannot
Perceive such bliss as in your
Frozen warmth does shine.

Your strict and aged
Sweetness mine—how
Fondness grows in hurt
As in most compromising love.

Endless Rains

The rains fall deep to wash
All man's concern; the drudgery,
The dragging days that pass like fire—
Speed their way to other days when
We no more; when fluid dirt, these
Short, cold days, my days of angry,
Fearful sadness pass and passed
I too shall be. Wipe the fear again,
Swallow that sweet, shrinking pride;
That confidence once had: now
Almost bare, invisible to me.

Night brings the pour of icy
Liquid from a starless sky—
Again I breath: deep the
Hurt and deep the pain;
To pray these endless
Rains do wash my
Sickness dry, before
I die in flooded misery,
In lonely silence.

Hail this day that brings
More rain, more joy—
A fitted, perfect match
For stolen years, for
Spent emotion. In headless
Trust those shiny lies
Now shimmer cold like
Glassy eyes of broken
Hearts and faltered dreams.

Harsh Passage

Fine your sacred word
That closed the door
To reason, that made a
Harboured knowledge mine.

Thrown against the time
Of beaten flame, of ashy will—
Landed on a slate hearth with
Temper lost and thrown.

I keep these thoughts a private
Realm that has no exit, beats my
Sheltered skin and rakes a
Mindless afternoon
To neat condition.

Trail me not, sweet stranger—
Think your thoughts and
Live your share of grief,
When tried in tense
Frustration, will I
Take my punishment
As man—most understood,
Most misconstrued.

The oddity of observation,
As we differ so; whose
Happy cause stands naked
Trial on my skeletal redemption;
By the skin of justice are we
Burned through our adulthood.

Appetite of Few

One day the phone calls stopped:
Where limousines once reigned;
A little quiet sadness (in times
Of soft, affectioned grief) did
Give to strangers utter glad
And satisfactory retreat.

We sipped the bitterness with
Aged wine, we lost the
Fervor of first years and
When the moon no longer
Dazzled us, we chose to walk
The beat; to run, to fly, to
Scale success in all its madness—
Graved by single feats, by
Unpretentious reason.

Those sneers of prickled luck
That through my heart once
Pierced, now made a hole
Of burned emotion reach this
New, this candid trick.

Lost to books of nothing worth,
Sold to wild imaginations; sit
And drink your hater's words
As but an appetite of few.

We know each other's fated
Try, so single—burn your
Fortune at the stake: my love
Is wounded, brother; we
Will meet in heaven yet.

Remembered Well

In noble reverence you stood,
So preached as would the
Highest order want and
Told in song a tale as long
As all eternity forgotten.

Around you gathered
Even folk—from walks
Diverse, from ancients
Found; in you surround
Their magic felt on this
Sweet, charitable night.

Together hands, in verse
As love did fold a perfumed
Table round; with music's
Vapors well-rehearsed,
Applauded you shall stand.

Amid the brotherhood so
Felt in turn from kind, from
Keen, from young and old.
A word is passed, a meal
Prepared: when in so
Mild a vision just, remains
A treasure for the year—
Remembered well in
Sacred realm.

For gratitude we pause a state,
To breathe the brisk and frozen
Air—outside an endless star
Does shine on your embracing call.

The windy corners where,
Behind an iron frame of
Glass doors, I looked-out
In sweet expectation;
Today revealed became
In one such instant flash:

As strangers passed my
Heart; to pierce this
Life in quickest flurry—
Scattered then like lonely
Wreaths on frozen graves,
In winter's solemn glory.

Praise the years when
Luck became us, soft the
Tender passage crossed—
Into a wishful contemplation,
Sadness streams no more.

*Nothing to
Our Hands*

Elephant tears that
Shine in the night
And swell these lids
To see no tomorrow;
In bleak, grey cold
Will pass these days
Like endless Englands
Here: Scattered 'cross
A semi-frozen land.

New land with new thoughts—
Still the old, sweet troubles
Sweat us out and you, who
Go in optimism, look to
Change the system rich;
To teach, to govern well.

Who sees it done in this
One hundred—now we
Near the end: where you
Can emulate the poor and
Look to once defend a
Wealth begotten. Only we,
With nothing to our hands
And everything in open sight,
Are so in your eyes blessed.

Can this be true redemption
As we suffer for the
Wills of man and live
Now rid of power,
Void of truth—
Virtue our only friend.

Liaisons' lust that sets into
These aging skins—
Dare not speak, there is no
Cause today which can come
Close to justify your wins.

Loose the fight
With victor's eyes
And turn your head
Away in shame; where
Kindly anger once revenge
Did take, now sends these
Vacant spirits high.

A Constant Deed

Imagination's sweet embrace
Does shine to me each day
In tainted glory, reach my
Heart in full caress and
Pat my shoulder.

Instead the real ambition
Turns to scorn a constant
Deed, to rule this lonely
Observation, to entice
A worldly knowledge lost
In drudgery of daily toil.

The face of beauty bronzed
And free, once radiant in
Summer's joy, now stands
A painted farce in expectation
Of a morsel thrown to much
Appease one's conscience.

Alone, surrounded by a
Million stars; outshined
With multitudes of promises,
Outlived by folly, wishes
Made and friends unknown
To keep us company, to
Hide our woes.

Keep silent now, for in a
Word ungrateful labeled
Will we charged be and
Even this (not ours)
Destiny, might too
Be taken from us.

Cry This
Night Away

Green the growth of human kind—
Invention's passive reign does pass
To tranquil harmony's enchanted
Prowess; in a silent breeze, in
Children's tapered laughter, as
In exuberance of innocent relief.

The amber wood, the rustling branch,
The minion's grand allure now dwarfed
By softened joy and selfless love. Hot
Freedom fights the shore, a lucky few
Again receive their due— when likeness
In these tropical enchantments probes
A futile remedy, we shine in night's
Sweet sweat; we call our futures bright.

We live so prone to consequence,
So quenched in hard critique, so
Dampened in a resurrected wetness;
Cry this night away to fill another
Light, another swift acknowledgment.

Spec of Life

Each year comes with a
Tearful pleasure—of days
Gone wild in work, as nights
Forgotten on a fearful quest;
Of answers lost when moments
Gathered for a second youth,
A trifle weathered.

Each year goes with a
New beginning, a new
Endeavour, a newer thought
To bring-in joy to solemn
Moments passed by
Hopes, by truths.

Now look again to see
A crumbling vision in
The spec of life—each
Year goes by in resonance,
In trying night, in headless
Folly. How pains the
Listener to stop and hear,
A once-forgotten heart,
An earnest dream.

Remember as each year
Goes into history, we lonely
One and all shall stand in perfect
Harmony tonight: when that old
Whistle blows-in yet another year,
another set of instruments to guide us
Blindly to the final punctuation.

Set this sun into my
Summer's golden lights
And bury deep each passive
Sigh of recognition lost, of
Contradiction born. Say
Free we roam a powdered
Dream that wakes us for the
Ringing false alarm and raises
Mute another happy year.

*Lives
Undone*

The ghosts of lost children,
Who peer-out from the
Shadows of a photograph—
To show their glory, their
Forgiveness. They, the souls
Unknown, forgotten; trust
Our freedom for their own.

We lost receivers—
Unidentified, un-made;
Choose to flesh ourselves
In virtue: yet in us, these
Little lives un-done, become
Before the eyes of time and
In a smaller weakness. They
(Over-shadowed by a
Morsel of acknowledgment)
Grow live, grow strength
Bewildered, grow to be what
Hindered once was made.

Then little only are they
In the briefest time, that
To their nameless
Presence given, now in
Trying pleasure found.

The Only
Truth

For you, the springing youth—
Of intellect unbound, these
Simple verse may written be.
In such medieval times might
Wed to strangers gone in years,
Now birth of children born in
Cruel circumstance are subject
To our politics' appeal—gain
Reason, gain your solid depth:
Which in each heart does lie
And this, the only truth we know,
May in your present fortune shine.

True Will

54

To think of the world as it
Passes and everything in it —
The stars, as the cosmos: an
Endless, black night adorned in
Perfection above and around;
So low that these specs of
New life and of old reach
The ends of the earth.

And you my sweet sage,
My only true will of complete,
Earnest sentiment; deeds are
Your word, my humble protector.
To your gentle wisdom I count-out
My days and tribute adoring cannot
Find the ways to justly repay the
Endless array of your kindness.

Though ceaseless the trying,
Though fruitful my quest—
In you there is excellence
Well at its best—that flesh
Can uphold it and soul efforts
Try, still you as a person:
So perfect you are!

True
Condition

Remember being here—
Naked, crying: a stranger
Walking-in on me; sitting,
(Just another muse) exuding
Sounds ethereal—of passions
Verse, ignored with null voice,
Not asked opinion, valued none;
Those days still fresh inside my
Heart, the hurt they bashed
Upon this youth.

Not yours nor mine,
It lasts a trifle known
In years—how now
With seeds revealed has
Changed this harsh-admitted,
True condition. Now alone:
A custom made can soothe
The life immediate.

The Gift

When nothing's yours
In realms of reach,
The gift most sure
Comes felt, not preached—
A heart in trust and
Promise kept is all
A tribute I can let.

To your sweet name,
To earnest love, to every
Wish of kindness fair:
I give my life instead
Of gold and keep each
Word a gift untold.

Time Alone

I wish to read you every story
And by such honour, flattered be—
But time alone holds key to hatred
As to benevolence, my dream;

So let together all these strangers
Hold damnation free. Let cruelty
Ride blind, un-noticed in a world
Of talents' spree and let the winter
Suns rejoice abundant while angry
Spirits perish in a suffocating stew.

Our love, alone by worldly pleasures
Tarnished, though to a love as pure—
This cannot be. Wipe clean the slate
Of bitter conscience and leave
Behind a vanished history.

Though far, so far in distant
Worlds the spirit floats—
A candle lit with prayer
Sheds light on those sharp
Elements now little known.

The evident has faces few;
They steer us ways their
Own. In heart's pure, only
Challenge—still the truth
With piercing love does
Hide in its most obvious.

A force contented with,
That learns the taste of
Damp confusion; holds
The breath of reason
When it sees such
Hiding and such fear.

Bow low to torn emotion,
Stand head-strong when
The muscle flexed of
Vivid blows (to none
Deserved) does show
Itself in public scorn.

Rise the Day

High treason and elation
Such as Hamlet staged
His widowed kin—
Directed at the humored
Lot of angels standing
At attention.

Happy, sweet attention
With the gentle taste of
Love still on the lips
Of demons. Rise the
Day to mild correction,
Guide-on way that
Charted-out before
And step not from the
Given path adorned.

50 *Years*

I read your heart
And thought it fair—
An imprint left already there;
To have this evident impulse
To find a worthy watch of
Gold—to mark your day, to
Justly serve this decade new.

Presented here, in humble
Shyness words encrusted,
Love held strong. Though
What you have already
Long is in my eyes such
Beauty made: a match
To this is unattained.

Now wear whatever please
Your will; if none, its honour
Still to give! Be sure I know
And always keep the gentle
Truth where your heart sleeps.

When you awake, my tale
Will tell; our children often
Ask to hear and you with us
Together stay for years ahead:
And days like these we cherish.

On Performance

The dread of stage:
As joy to artists hiding,
Peering from their easel—
This duty to performance
Pursues each step of life;
No change in destiny
Can shake it from a
Raveled sleeve or
Evening coat's perfection.

Play the harmonies sublime
To front both lover, critic;
Speak in sounds ethereal—
Stutter, then forget.

Join together confidence
To brave the weathers
Of dispute; exercise
This likeliness to crumble
Or to keep strong guard
On meek anxieties and
Lead them to a conquered test.

Sweet Day

The call we cannot make—
To those we love, who
Walk with us, in us;
No longer are a part
Of life, no longer
Stand by us to
Guide, to fight.

We fight alone,
We stand and
Give the way to
Power, judgment, glory.

Rise to meet
This calling day
When we to friends
Do give our hearts, when
In a lost, sweet notion
Fall again and (over our)
Truths so fall with us.

Sweet day of bitter lies,
The day when all we
Worthy givers give alike
And die. What day is this
We know so well!

A Season Wild was designed at The Oliphant Press, New York City, and printed in an edition of five hundred copies. The cover illustration is by Abraham Brewster. The typeface used is Centaur. All papers used in the book are recycled.